GUIDE
TO
SMALL CLAIMS
IN THE COUNTY COURT

MICHAEL MAJOR
EASYWAY GUIDES

3

Easyway Guides
38 cromwell road
Walthamstow
London 17 9JN

© Easyway Guides 1997

ISBN 1900694 25 5

A British Library Cataloguing in Publication data record is available
for this title from the British Library.

The author and publisher acknowledge that the law may change from
time to time and render certain information in this book obsolete.
Whislst all care has been taken to achieve accuracy, the author and
publisher cannot accept responsibility for any errors or ommissions
within.

Cover design by Straightforward Graphics
Printed in England by BPC Wheaton Ltd, Exeter.

CONTENTS

INTRODUCTION

This book is designed to help and assist those people who are considering taking action in the small claims division of the county court, or who are being sued in the county court.

The book will also be invaluable to the student of law, the practitioner and the adviser and indeed anyone else who wishes to further their knowledge of the small claims court and how to take action.

The book takes a practical approach and deals first with the general areas of law likely to affect the individual when he or she wishes to take action aginst another, be it individual or company.

The rest of the book concentrates on taking the potential plaintiff (person taking action) through all the procedures up to the court stage and to representation and to the final order against the defendant.

The book also takes the defendants point of view as it is recognised that not all claims are just and people need advice on how to represent themselves.

More and more we are living in a climate where the individual is encouraged to take his or her own action. This book should greatly assist in that undertaking.

Good Luck!

CHAPTER ONE
SMALL CLAIMS

Almost all disputes which involve less than £3,000 are automatically referred to small claims arbitration.

THE RIGHTS OF SUPPLIERS AND CONSUMERS

Where goods are delivered or services rendered, the supplier or service provider is entitled to the agreed price or payment for the service rendered. The following situations apply:

When goods are supplied which do not comply with the contract, or in breach of terms implied by the Sale of Goods Act (see below), the purchaser is entitled to either compensation known as damages or if the breach is serious, to reject the goods and claim damages for financial loss, for example, a refund of the purchase price, or the cost above the agreed purchase price for goods within the terms of the contract, and any additional loss suffered. The compensation claimed would be the purchase price and any other additional loss suffered.

Sale of Goods Act 1979.

The Sale of Goods Act implies certain terms into contracts for the sale of goods. This means that the seller must supply goods which satisfy certain statutory terms of contract imposed by Parliament. The principal implied terms are:-

the vendor must own the goods or have the right to sell them;

if the goods are sold by description they must correspond with that description. This applies to goods which are described in some way by a label or a notice identifying the kind of goods they are, or to specific goods which the buyer has not seen at the time of the contract and which are bought on the basis of a description;

where a seller sells goods in the course of a business the goods must be of satisfactory quality. This is defined as meaning that they must meet the standard that a reasonable person would regard as satisfactory, taking account of any description of the goods, the price (if relevant) and all the other relevant circumstances. The Act lists the following as aspects of the quality of goods; the fitness for the purpose for which goods of the kind in questions are commonly supplied, the appearance and finish, freedom from minor defects, safety and durability. These provisions do not apply to goods of unsatisfactory quality if the fault has been specifically drawn to the buyer's attention before the contract is made;

if the goods are sold by sample the bulk must correspond to the sample in quality and be free from any defect which would not be apparent on reasonable examination of the sample.

If these conditions are not satisfied, the purchaser has the rights specified above, to damages, to rejection and damages, or to affirm the contract and claim damages for loss suffered.

Supply of Goods and Services Act, 1982

This Act relates to the supply of services which includes a vast range of activities, from having your house altered or redecorated, to having your hair dyed, to having your coat dry cleaned. It includes the supply of goods because often when services are supplied the materials required are also supplied such as paint for decorating, and these materials must be of a suitable standard.

The supplier of services is entitled to payment of his invoice and if a price has not been agreed he is entitled to a reasonable charge. Even if the work is not of a reasonable standard the supplier may be entitled to a reasonable payment.

Where a service is supplied by someone acting in the course of a business then purchaser is entitled to receive a service performed with reasonable care and skill and carried out within a reasonable time. If goods are supplied they must be of satisfactory quality and correspond to any description or sample by which they have been sold. If the work or goods are not of a reasonable standard the purchaser must prove that this is the case and may claim the remedies mentioned above. For example a purchaser may be entitled to damages if the work is so sub-standard that financial loss is suffered such as for plumbing or re-wiring which needs to be completely re-done or a coat which needs to be replaced after cleaning.The Supply of Goods and Services Act also applies to contracts for the hire of goods although not to hire purchase agreements. Like contracts for sale, contracts for hire have terms implied into them that the supplier of the goods (the bailor) has the right to hire them out, that they correspond to any description or sample by reference to which the contract has been made and that where the goods are supplied in the course of business they will be of satisfactory quality. In addition, there is an implied term that the person who hires the goods (the bailee) will enjoy quiet possession of the goods for the agreed period unless they are taken by the owner or another person with a right or charge over them which the bailee was told or knew about before the contract was made.

Quantum Meruit

This is a legal rule which is derived from previous cases rather than the supply of goods and services statute. It translates as "as much as he deserves" and means that if one party is prevented by the other, in breach of the contract, from completing the work he had contracted to perform then he may claim payment for what he has already done on a quantum meruit basis. A claim can also be made where partial performance has been voluntarily accepted by the other party.

Cheques

If goods or services are paid for by a cheque which is subsequently dishonoured the recipient can base his claim on the cheque and does not have to prove the contract which led to its payment. This is because the cheques, bills of exchange and promissory notes are regarded as independent contracts, separate from the contract for sale. Consequently there are only a few grounds on which a defendant can defend such a claim such of fraud, duress, total failure of consideration and possibly misrepresentation.

Unfair Contract Terms Act, 1977

Contracts often include exclusion clauses, where one side attempts to limit its liability or the rights of the other party in the event of a breach of contract. The Unfair Contract Terms Act makes any clause excluding or limiting liability for death or personal injury void. Any exclusion clause which restricts or limits the terms implied by the Sale of Goods Act, where one party is dealing as a consumer, is void. This means that the exclusion has no effect. Any exclusion clause where one party is dealing on standard terms or one party is a business, will only be effective in so far as the person relying on it can prove that it is "reasonable" as defined by the Act which means that the term "shall have been a fair and reasonable one to be included having regard to the circumstances which were, or ought reasonably to have been known to or in the contemplation of the parties when the contract was made". It is for the person alleging that a term or notice is reasonable to show that it is.

Personal injury

Personal injury claims are treated differently to other claims in that they are not automatically referred to arbitration if the damages claimed exceed £1,000. This is because personal injury cases often raise difficult issues and the parties are more likely to need legal advice and representation the cost of which is not recoverable in small claims.

There has been some doubt about whether the £1,000 limit relates just to damages you are claiming for the physical injury itself or whether additional claims for things such as loss of earnings or the cost of treatment can be used to bring the claim over the arbitration limit. It seems that the £1,000 limit relates to the claim as a whole including the additional damages.Personal injuries can have been caused deliberately but in most cases the Plaintiff seeks to prove that the defendant was negligent. Four points must be proved to establish negligence:

that the defendant owed a duty of care. With regard to personal injuries everyone should take reasonable care to avoid doing things

or failing to do things which they can reasonably foresee would be likely to injure people who they ought reasonably to have foreseen as being so affected by their acts or omissions.

the defendant acted in breach of his duty

the breach caused the plaintiffs injury, and

the injury was reasonably foreseeable, and not a freak accident

if the plaintiff was also negligent the court may find that he was guilty of contributing negligence and reduce the damages he receives to reflect the extent to which he was responsible for causing his own injuries.

In the case of injury at work, the plaintiff could also claim compensation on the grounds that the defendant acted in breach of a statutory duty, of which there are many imposed by the Health & Safety At Work legislation.

These areas are complicated and research should be undertaken before taking legal action. However, in legal terms, a simple case could well be suited to the small claims procedure.

Consumer Protection Act 1977

This Act allows action against a producer of goods which are unsafe and cause personal injury or loss of or damage to property provided the value of the claim is over £275, excluding interest. The term producer includes the manufacturer,anyone who holds himself out as the producer by putting his name or trade mark on the product and an importer of the product into a Member State of the European Community from a place outside the EC in order to supply it to another in the course of his business. The Act does not apply to damage to the defective product itself or damage to any product supplied with a defective component comprised in it. Furthermore, there is no liability unless the product is a type of property ordinarily intended for private use, occupation or consumption and was intended by the Plaintiff mainly for such purposes. A person who suffers damage to his business property must therefore sue on a contract or in negligence.

THE OCCUPIERS LIABILITY ACT

The 1957 Act governs the liability of an occupier in respect of personal injury or damage to property suffered by those who come lawfully onto his premises as visitors. An occupier is under a duty to take such care as in all circumstances of the case is reasonable, to see that the visitor will be reasonably safe in using the premises for the purpose for which he is invited or is permitted to be there. An occupier can discharge his duty by warning his visitor of the particular danger provided that the warning is sufficient to enable the visitor to be reasonably safe.

The 1984 Act concerns the liability of an occupier with regard to people other than his visitors in respect of injuries suffered on the premises due to the state of the premises or things done or omitted to be done on them. This includes trespassers and people exercising private rights of way but not those using public rights of way. The occupier owes such people a duty if he is aware of a danger or has reasonable grounds to believe one exists, if he knows or has reasonable grounds to believe that the non-visitor is in the vicinity of the danger concerned or that he may come into the vicinity and the risk is one against which in all the circumstances of the case he may reasonably be expected to offer the non-visitor some protection. An occupier may be able to discharge his duty by taking reasonable steps to warn people of the danger but whether the warning is adequate will depend on the circumstances.

Other

This includes a wide variety of things many but not all of which are based on breach of contract. Examples include non payment of rent, failure to return a deposit, housing disrepair, illegal eviction, nuisance from noisy neighbours, harassment and so on. In this area rather than just seeking damages people may wish to apply for an injunction or an order for specific performance. This is where a court orders a person to do something or to refrain from doing something. For example, to repair a house or to refrain from disturbing their neighbours or to comply with the terms of an agreement. Up to ,260 may be awarded for legal advice obtained in order to bring or defend a small claim for either an injunction or specific performance or similar relief but this does not cover the cost of being represented at the hearing.

Limitation Periods

The law imposes time limits, known as limitation periods within which you must commence your case. Time begins to run from the date of the breach of contract or the date of the actionable tort. Tort includes claims for negligence which are not based on breach of contract, nuisance and occupiers liability. In personal injury cases it runs from the date when the injury was sustained or, if it is later from the date when the plaintiff first knew of their injuries. The court has a discretion to extend the time .vailable in personal injury cases in certain circumstances.

The time limits are:

Contract 3 years

Tort   6 years

Defective products (Consumer Protection Act 1987) 3 years

Personal injury   3 years

If you are the Defendant and the Plaintiff's claim is out of time you will have a defence to the claim but it is important that you mention it on your defence form as it is not automatic.

What is and is not a small claim?

Claims for the possession of land cannot be dealt with under the small claims procedure.

Employment disputes such as claims for unfair dismissal and sexual or racial discrimination are dealt with by Industrial Tribunals.

Because legal aid is not available for small claims and your costs are not normally recoverable if you win, there is an incentive for plaintiffs with claims near the upper limit to inflate their claims to over £3,000. However the court regards this as a misuse of process which justifies restricting a successful plaintiff's costs to those he would have recovered under the small claims procedure. In these circumstances the Plaintiff is likely to have incurred more costs than he would have done if he had brought the case as a small claim and will have to pay them

15

himself even if he wins his case. The test the court applies is "could the Plaintiff reasonably expect to be awarded more than £3,000?".

If you are a defendant faced with what you regard as an inflated claim you should state in your defence that the claim cannot reasonably exceed £3,000 and should be automatically referred to arbitration.

Where a claim is referred for arbitration a district judge may order that it should not be treated as a small claim and there should be a trial in court instead if:

> the case raises a difficult question of law or a complex question of fact or;
>
> fraud is alleged against any party or;
>
> the parties agree that the case should be tried in court or;
>
> it would not be reasonable for the case to proceed as a small claim having regard to its subject matter, the size of any counterclaim and the circumstances of the parties or the interests of any other person likely to be affected by the award.

The judge can do this on his own initiative or in response to an application by any party.

CHAPTER TWO
BEFORE LEGAL ACTION

Obviously it is desirable to avoid litigation if at all possible and the best way to do this is to prevent claims arising in the first place.

If you intend to employ someone to perform a service obtain estimates beforehand outlining exactly what is to be done and how much it will cost. It is also wise to ask if the people you are doing business with belong to any professional or trade associations. Write and confirm all the details of the contract before the work begins.

If you run a business, consider the benefits of a credit reference agency to check the creditworthiness of new customers. Reports can be obtained on-line via a computer and modem, for example, from Prestel. Depending on the service you are buying, ensure that you have a written contract or that you use your standard terms of business in a sale or purchase.

If you run a business and encounter serious problems in paying your creditors, always negotiate terms of payment and discuss your situation openly and honestly. Such action at an early stage often avoids legal proceedings being taken against you. Always keep your bank manager informed and up to date with your business affairs and avoid giving him unexpected surprises.

Ensure that you keep all relevant documents, such as a receipt for a payment, the contract guarantees, delivery note or any letters written. Also keep a copy of any advertisement you relied on in entering into a contract. If you speak to anyone on the telephone, make a record of the person's name and of what was said. A case often turns on the documentary evidence available at the arbitration hearing and relevant documents with which you may have use to prove a case to the satisfaction of a judge usually come into existence before of during a dispute.

The small claims court should be viewed as a last resort. Before issuing a Summons, make a clear complaint and attempt to reach a compromise by contacting the defendant. If no compromise or settlement is achieved, before issuing a Summons, you should write to the defendant threatening legal action and stating the recompense you are demanding. This is known as a A letter before action. It is important to keep a copy of this and of all correspondence.

Before taking someone to court

Before issuing a summons to enforce a debt or payment of an invoice, etc., consider whether the defendant is worth suing. A credit reference agency will be able to give you some idea of the creditworthiness of a potential defendant or you can check the register of county court judgments.

CHAPTER THREE

PROCEDURE

When a county court summons for £3,000 or less is issued, the dispute is a small claim and is automatically referred by the Court to Arbitration. This in an informal procedure where a Judge hears each side of a dispute in a private room, rather than in an Open Court. Solicitors fees are not awarded to the successful party to an Arbitration - unlike a hearing in Open Court. This is to encourage members of the public to conduct their own case.

The Court provides standard forms for completion by the opponents throughout a case with the intention that for simple matters, you could present your own case.

The steps you must take to begin a County Court action against another person(s) are as follows:

The Summons

A summons is a document which is used to start proceedings in the County Court. In small claims cases it is a form which the Plaintiff fills in. The next Chapter will tell you in detail how to do this. A summons form can be obtained from the Court Office. When you have completed the form two copies of the Summons must be taken to the Court Office and the Court Fee paid (see appendix for fees). The court will then serve the Summons on the Defendant with three forms, a Form of Admission (N9A), a form for filing a Defence (N9B) and a form for filing a Counterclaim (N9B). The Court will also:

> post a form called a "Plaint Note" (N205A) to you. This form records the details of the claim, the case number and date of service. The case number is now the reference point for your case and no steps can be taken without quoting it

> you will also receive a Request for Judgment which is attached to the Plaint Note.

To claim damages two types of Summons are available, they are:

> a Summons claiming a fixed sum of money, known as a "liquidated demand" - Form N1, or

> a Summons claiming damages to be assessed, where the court must assess and determine the level of compensation payable - Form N2.

The court will post the Summons to the Defendant with a Form of Admission, Defence and Counterclaim.

The Summons used in small claims is described as a "Default Summons". This is a summons used to start a "default action". The significance of the term "default" is that, if the Defendant does not file a defence, the court will order judgment in the Plaintiff's favour without a hearing. In other words, by issuing a default summons, the

Defendant is summonsed to answer the Plaintiff's claim and if he fails to do so by not filing a defence, the court will order judgment for the Plaintiff. In the case of a claim for a fixed amount, the court will order payment of that amount. If the amount is not specified, the court will order judgment for the Plaintiff with damages to be assessed. A hearing date will be set for the assessment of damages.

Defence and Counterclaim

The Defendant must return the Form of Admission (N9A), Defence and Counterclaim (N9B) to the Court within 14 days of the date of service printed on the summons. The Defendant has the following options:

Admission or Partial Admission

The Defendant may admit the whole claim by posting the Form of Admission direct to the Plaintiff. He can also make a request for time to pay. The Plaintiff must then either accept or reject the request returning the Form of Admission to the court office with the Request for Judgment. The Court will enter judgment but if the suggested method of payment is rejected, the Court will enter judgment and set a date for a hearing to consider the method of payment.

If the Defendant admits part of the claim, and the plaintiff does not accept the sum offered, the offer may be rejected and the Defendant must file a defence in respect of the balance. The court will set a date for an arbitration hearing.

Defence

If the Defendant files a Defence, the Plaintiff will receive a copy from the Court and the case will be transferred to the Defendant's local court which will set a date for the Arbitration Hearing.

If you are a Plaintiff and you expect the Defendant to file a defence, you will save time if you issue your Summons in his local County Court.

If a Defence is not filed within 14 days of service, the Plaintiff may return the Request for Judgment, and Judgment-in-Default will be entered in his favour. He will then receive a copy of the Judgment which will be in the form of an order for immediate payment or payment by instalments. This may be set aside on certain grounds which are discussed later.

Counterclaim

The Defendant's counterclaim is a claim made by the Defendant against the Plaintiff which may be less than his claim, so his claim is reduced, or it may be greater. A counterclaim is a separate action. Rather than the Defendant issuing his own Summons, the dispute is managed in one set of proceedings by the defendant issuing a counterclaim. The Plaintiff is entitled to file a defence to the counterclaim. However, the Plaintiff is treated as having denied the allegations made in a counterclaim if a defence is not filed. Judgment-in-default is therefore not applicable to a counterclaim.

Date of the Hearing

If a defence is filed, the court will set a date for the arbitration and issue directions - you will be notified by Form N18A. The Court must :

> give not less than 14 days notice of the date of the hearing, and
>
> issue directions before any hearing or pre-hearing.

Directions Issued by the Court

When you are notified of the date of the hearing, you will also receive directions, these are the courts instructions as to how the case should proceed. District Judges have wide powers to issue directions and local

courts have their own practise. The purpose of directions is to ensure that the arbitration runs smoothly. The directions for an arbitration printed on Form N18A are usually limited to two:

> not less than 14 days before the date fixed for the hearing, each party must post to the other copies of any documents they intend to rely on at the hearing, and
>
> not less than 7 days before the hearing, a copy of any expert report on which each party intends to rely must be posted to both the court and the other party

this process of exchanging documents is known as disclosure of evidence.

Enforcement Proceedings

If the Defendant does not comply with the Judgment, which is a Court Order, you will be entitled to take enforcement proceedings which are discussed further on in this book.

CHAPTER FOUR
COMPLETING A SUMMONS

Use Form N1 if you are claiming a fixed sum (known as a liquidated demand) for example a debt, a dishonoured cheque, or to claim a refund for faulty goods. Use Form N2 in cases where the amount of money claimed needs to be assessed (known as unliquidated damages) for example in a personal injury claim.

The Plaintiff's Name and Address

The summons form requires the plaintiff's full name and address. If the plaintiff is a company give the address of the registered office. If it is a firm write "a firm" after the name. If you are an individual trading under another name write your name and then "trading as" and the name you use. If the plaintiff is under 18 he is a minor and so may bring an action for unpaid wages himself but for all other actions he must sue by a representative known as a "next friend" usually an adult relative or friend. In such cases Form number N235 is used.

Is the correct person is bringing the action? For example if a friend gave you some goods as a present which turn out to be faulty and you want a refund of the purchase price, then the person who actually bought the goods should be the one to bring the court action.

This is because it is the purchaser who is a party to the contract which has been breached not the recipient of the gifts and only parties to the contract can sue for its breach. This rule is known as the doctrine of privity of contract.

Part 2 is for if you want the court papers to be sent to you at a different address from the one given in Part 1. It is normally only completed if a solicitor is acting on your behalf.

Defendants Name and Address

The defendant's full name and address should be given. If you do not know their full name write Mr. or Ms and give their surname and their initials if you know them. If it is a company, firm or using the trading name see the comments in relation to plaintiffs above. If the defendant is a company the address of its registered office will be on its headed notepaper or you can find it out by telephoning Companies House in Cardiff.

If the defendant is a minor they will need to be represented in the case by someone known as their "guardian ad litem" usually a parent or other adult relative or friend. A summons should not be sent directly to the minor but instead should be sent to the parent or guardian or other adult who will be acting for them.

Type of Claim

A brief description of what type of claim you are making is required in the next space. This means stating what the claim consists of for example, breach of contract, non-payment of invoice or bad workmanship.

Particulars of Claim

The particulars or details of your claim must be set out in the largest box or on a separate piece of paper. It is important to use numbered paragraphs and to set out each point relevant to your case. For example in a contract claim you must state or "plead" the following:

if it is relevant say who the parties are;

that there was a contract and when it was made, was it written or oral, can it be implied from letters and similar documents?

the relevant terms of the contract including implied terms. For example terms implied by the Sale of Goods Act;

that you have performed all or part of your side of the contract or why you have not done so;

that the contract has been breached and give details of what the defendant has done or failed to do that puts him in breach;

what damage you have suffered as a result of the defendants breach.

Lastly, you must state what you claim; for example payment of an invoice (state the amount) and interest at the contractual or statutory rate.

If your claim is in tort rather than contract for example you are saying that the defendant was negligent, then you must plead the following:

who the parties are (if relevant)

describe the accident or event which is the basis of your complaint and say when it took place

that the accident or act you are complaining about was caused by the defendant's negligence or breach of duty and give details

that you suffered damage as a result of the facts alleged and give details of all the damage

Finally, state what you are claiming by either giving a figure or saying that you would like the damages to be assessed. Claim interest.

You should then sign underneath the particulars.

Next?

Take the two copies of the completed summons form to the court and pay the issue fee. The court may ask for copies. The court will stamp the summons form and post it to the defendant with forms of admission, defence and counterclaim, explained in the next chapter. The defendant must reply to your summons within 14 days from the date of service printed on the Plaint Note. A company has 16 days to reply.

If the Defendant files a defence, the court will post a copy to you. A form of Admission is returned direct to the Plaintiff.

Obtaining Judgment in Default

You will receive a Plaint Note from the Court with a Request for Judgment-in-Default attached (Form N18A). If a defence is not filed (you will know because the court will inform you if one is received), complete and return the Request for Judgment to the court.

Accepting an Admission and Offer of Payment

The court serves a summons on the defendant with a form of Admission Defence and Counterclaim. If the defendant admits the claim, the form of admission is posted direct to you, the plaintiff. You must then complete and return it to the court requesting judgment and an order for payment. You may request judgment but object to the method of payment, or accept a part admission but pursue the balance in respect of which the defendant should file a defence and/or counterclaim.

If the Defendant admits the claim but asks for time to pay, you may reject the proposal. In the event of a dispute, the court staff will set an amount with reference to the information supplied by the defendant. The order to pay is issued on form N30(2), but if you object to the level of instalments, you are entitled to make an application to the district judge using form N244 for him to set a level of instalments. the case is then transferred to the defendant's local court for a hearing.

29

CHAPTER FIVE
THE DEFENDANTS RESPONSE

A Summons is served by the court with forms for Admission, Defence and Counterclaim.

If you do not reply by returning the form of Admission or Defence and Counterclaim the plaintiff will be entitled to request judgment against you by returning the request he will have attached to the Plaint Note. The court will then enter "judgment-in-default" against you which means that the court will order you to either:

> pay the liquidated sum demanded, or;

> in the case of an unliquidated sum, judgment will be entered against you but with damages to be assessed, with reference to the evidence given by the Plaintiff at the hearing.

If judgment in default is entered against you you must either have it set aside or pay the sum demanded. If a judgment debt is not paid a record of the fact is kept by the court on the Register of County Court Judgments for six years. This register can be referred to by people who want to know if you are creditworthy consequently you may have trouble obtaining credit or goods on hire purchase.

The effect of filing a Defence to a Default Summons is that a hearing will be ordered and the plaintiff loses the right to judgment in default.

Admission

If you admit the claim for the sum demanded, you may complete the form of Admission and post it to the Plaintiff:

> with payment, or

> with an offer for payment by instalments.

The effect of an admission is that the plaintiff will be entitled to judgment in respect of the amount you admit. The issue then is the method of payment and whether the plaintiff or the court will permit payment by instalments. It is possible just to admit part of the claim if you believe that the plaintiff is not entitled to the whole amount but in such a case, you must use the forms of defence and/or counterclaim to deny that you owe the balance of the claim. If an admission is filed but the Plaintiff does not accept your offer to pay by instalments, the court staff will set an amount with reference to the information you supply. The order to pay is issued on form N30(2), but if you object to the level of instalments, you are entitled to make an application to the district judge using form N244 for him to set a different level of instalments. The case is then transferred to your local court for a hearing.

Defence

If you deny that the Plaintiff's claim is valid you must file a defence. However you can only file a defence if you have a reason for disputing the plaintiff's claim and not just a reluctance to pay him. Examples are that work done was faulty, the wrong goods were supplied and that the debt is really owed to another person. You should also file a defence if you admit art of the claim and the Plaintiff will not accept your offer of part ayment in full settlement. You must say why you do not owe the full mount.

reparing a Defence

ry and write your defence in numbered paragraphs.

ook very carefully at the plaintiff's claims. Go through his paragraphs ethodically and try to respond to every allegation by denying it, dmitting it or saying that you do not know. If you deny something then e plaintiff must prove the allegation. If you admit something it means at the plaintiff does not have to prove that particular point and the court ill take it as accepted.

is important to also put forward your side of the story summarising what ally happened and why it means you are not liable to the Plaintiff as they aim. However, remember that if you are making a claim of your own gainst the plaintiff, for example for damages,then the allegations that late to this should be made in the counter claim and not in the defence.

s well as putting forward an alternative version or interpretation of vents you can also take issue with the amount of damage the plaintiff aims to have suffered. For example you might say that goods which ere damaged are not as valuable as the plaintiff claims or his injury was ot as serious as the plaintiff suggests. You are also entitled to expect a aintiff to mitigate these losses. This means that they should take all asonable steps to minimise the loss caused even if there has been fault n the part of the defendant, for example by breach of contract. They

33

cannot recover loss which the defendant can prove resulted from a failur to mitigate. You can dispute the amount of loss suffered while sti denying that you were in any way responsible for any loss at all. This is prudent course of action as it may mean that

If you are unsuccessful in your defence you do not have to pay the fu amount the plaintiff is seeking.

The Form of Counterclaim

If you wish to make a claim against the Plaintiff, you may file counterclaim. This is equivalent to issuing your own summons against th plaintiff. Thus, while the defence answers the plaintiff's claim th counterclaim is a separate action, that will be considered with the origin claim. As with a plaintiff's original claim you request either a fixe amount as damages to be assessed. If the counterclaim is in excess of th small claims limit this does not prevent the case being automaticall referred to arbitration but it is one of the factors a district judge can tak into account when considering whether the case should proceed as a sma claim. A court fee will be payable if the counterclaim exceeds the clair against you.

A counterclaim should be made in the same way as the Particula contained in the Summons . Write in numbered paragraphs which sta clearly what you claim, why the plaintiff is liable and what compensatic you require. The plaintiff is entitled to file a Defence and Reply to counterclaim. It is advisable to do so especially if the counterclaim raises

1y new issues. However the allegations in a counterclaim are treated as enied even if a Defence and Reply is not filed.

etting Aside a Default Judgment

' a Default Judgment is made against you when you have a defence, you lay apply to the Court for the judgment to be "set aside" by using form 244, but you must establish grounds for the application, for example, lat you have a defence or that you did not receive the summons in the ost. The court will arrange an arbitration hearing. You must give :asons for your failure to file a defence and convince the judge that your :fence is genuine.

hird Party Proceedings

. defendant who holds a third party entirely or partly responsible for the laintiff's loss is entitled to join the third party in the action by issuing a hird Party Notice. Leave of the court is required to issue the Notice if the :fence has been filed.

n example of where you might want to join a third party is if the plaintiff rings an action seeking compensation for damage to his car caused by ou driving into the back of it. But you only hit the plaintiff's vehicle :cause your car was shunted forward as a result of being hit by a third arty's car. In such circumstances you would want the third party to be joined in the action as he is the person who is really responsible for the damage.

CHAPTER SIX
EVIDENCE

It is the responsibility of the parties to supply the evidence for the judge to consider.

Types of Evidence

Evidence is information which can be presented to the court to enable the judge to decide on the probability of a claim which has been made being correct or true. Evidence can take a number of different forms:

Oral Evidence. Both the plaintiff and the defendant will be able to give evidence by speaking to the District Judge, giving their account of events and presenting their arguments. They can also call witnesses to attend court and give oral evidence about any relevant fact of which they have knowledge. If a witness is unwilling to attend the hearing, you are entitled to compel their attendance by issuing a witness summons (Form N20). This must be done at least seven days before the hearing and it will mean that you have to pay the witnesses expenses and the cost of their travel to and from the court. Court staff will tell you how much this is. If you are successful and win the case you should be able to recover the cost of the witnesses travelling and overnight expenses reasonably incurred and for their loss of earnings from your opponent.

Witness Statements. Witnesses who can not come to the hearing can give their evidence in writing. They should give their full name and address and sign and date their statement. Such evidence can be very useful but, depending on the circumstances, it is likely to carry less weight than direct oral testimony because the other party and the judge do not have the opportunity to question the witness, and because seeing someone give their evidence would help the district judge to decide how credible he finds that witness. On the other hand, if you get your witness to make a statement prior to the hearing and ask your opponent if they will accept that the evidence contained in the statement is correct you may be able to save the cost and trouble of bringing the witness to court. Witness statements are also useful where you have a number of witnesses who are going to say the same thing. You can ask one of them to attend the hearing and request that the others make statements. Photocopies of witness statements should be given to the other party prior to the hearing in accordance with the court's directions.

Documentary Evidence. This includes things like letters, estimates, delivery notes, receipts, diary entries, guarantees and photographs. Judges are usually faced with parties giving contradictory oral evidence and the difficult job of choosing between them, so documentary evidence which supports one account rather than the other is very helpful. It is often a good idea to take photographs in preparation for the case.

In addition to documents you can use other physical evidence to support your claims. For example if the dispute is about reasonably small and portable goods you could take the goods in question, or a sample, along to the arbitration to show that they are faulty in some way. In some circumstances the arbitrator may want to visit the scene of the accident or the place where unsatisfactory work was done, or to go and see an object which cannot be brought to the court. This is known as a site visit and both the plaintiff and the defendant will be given notice in advance and the opportunity to attend.

Expert Evidence. This is required when it is necessary to decide a question which needs specialist or technical knowledge which the arbitrator is unlikely to have. For example a surveyor may give an opinion on building works and a doctor will be a suitable expert in personal injury cases. When a matter calls for expert evidence only a suitably qualified person can give it.

When you have found a suitable expert ask him to write a report. Explain clearly what you want and what is at issue This will ensure he answers the important questions and also that he does not do unnecessary work which will increase your costs. It may be possible for both you and your opponent to minimise your expenses by agreeing to use the same expert. In which case you should agree in advance what questions you want the expert to answer and what evidence he will see. Another alternative is for you to ask the court to appoint an expert to act as the arbitrator in place of the District Judge. In such circumstances you and your opponent would share the costs.If you already have a pre-arbitration appointment you can request that the District Judge agree to this procedure at that hearing. Alternatively you can apply on Form N244 and you will be given an appointment.

Remember to give copies of expert reports to your opponent and to the court before the arbitration date in accordance with the courts directions.

Onus of Proof

It is the Plaintiff who brings the case to court and who makes allegations about the defendant or his conduct and it is for the plaintiff to establish that these claims are true. In legal terms it is said that he bears the burden of proof.

Although the plaintiff formally bears the burden of proof, on a practical level both the plaintiff and the defendant can be subject to the "onus of proof". This means that when the plaintiff has made a plausible allegation and substantiated his claims, for example producing evidence that goods were delivered but not paid for then the onus is on the defendant to give an answer or give an explanation. The defendant might produce evidence of payment. This would then put the onus of proof back on the Plaintiff. The Plaintiff could allege that the payments were for other invoices and so on.

Because the plaintiff bears the burden of proof, if at the end of the hearing the arbitrator finds that the plaintiff's and the defendant's arguments are of equal strength he must decide in favour of the defendant and dismiss the summons. When he is making a counterclaim the defendant bears the burden of proof in respect of this part of the case.

Standard of Proof

It is unlikely that either party will be able to prove their case with certainty but this is not required. In order to discharge the burden of proof the plaintiff (or in a counterclaim the defendant) must show he is right "on the balance of probabilities".This means that the arbitrator must be satisfied that what he is claiming is more likely than not to be correct. The criminal standard of proof, that a case must be proved "beyond reasonable doubt" does not normally have any application in small claims.

What Must be Proven

At the hearing the plaintiff must prove each of the statements made in his particulars of claim. He must also prove the level of loss he has suffered because if he is successful the court will award damages to compensate him for his loss, not to punish the defendant. The plaintiff does not have to prove any of the particulars which are admitted by the defendant in his defence. It is also the plaintiff's responsibility to prove that the defendant received the summons. This is relevant when the defendant does not attend the hearing or attends but denies service, but it is not relevant when the defendant has returned one of the forms of admission, defence and counterclaim.

The Defendant must prove all of the allegations he makes in the counterclaim and the level of loss he suffered. He should also bring any evidence available to him which disproves or undermines any of the plaintiff's claims in the particulars of claim, including those about the extent of the loss he has suffered, or which supports the defendant's alternative account of events.

Rules of Evidence

The rules of evidence which normally govern what evidence is admissible, which means what the judge will consider and take into account, do not apply to small claims.

CHAPTER SEVEN
PREPARATION FOR A HEARING

The court controls what steps should be taken before the hearing by issuing "directions". However, sometimes these standard directions are not adequate. Either party can make an application to the court on form N244 for a preliminary appointment at which the party may request additional directions. This is not usually necessary in small claims proceedings but may be useful in complex cases such as personal injury claims. The other party may oppose your application or not attend the hearing. If at all possible try and agree the directions with your opponent then both parties can write to the court asking for the same direction. In nearly all cases, the court will grant any directions which both parties request.

A preliminary appointment can also be used to claim that the summons does not establish a claim as the defence does not present a proper defence. It would also be an opportunity to argue that claim does not really fall within the small claims limit or that it should be transferred to the county court for one of the other reasons outlined in chapter 1.

A preliminary appointment is informal and takes place in a private room with a district judge and the litigants present. Remember, a preliminary appointment is not the arbitration. Beyond establishing whether or not you have an arguable claim or defence the judge will not consider the merits of the case at this stage so you do not need to take along witnesses or to be fully prepared to argue your case at this stage.

Failure to attend appointment

If the plaintiff fails to attend, the judge will probably strike the case out. If the defendant does not attend, the judge could either issue direction or strike out the defence, or if the admission is filed, allow the plaintiff to prove the level of loss suffered.

If it has not done so already the court will set a date for the arbitration. If you cannot attend on the date set inform the court immediately. The judge who issues the directions will give a time estimate of how long he expects the case to last. If the time estimate is too short, write to the court and/or telephone the listings clerk because otherwise the judge may not have time to hear your case in full and you will have to go back on another date. Either the plaintiff or the defendant can ask for more time. Allow plenty of time for your witnesses to give their evidence and to be questioned by your opponent.

Complying with Directions

It is essential that you comply with the arbitrator's directions concerning what should be done and exchanged before the trial. Failure to exchange documentary evidence and expert reports may mean that you cannot use such evidence during the arbitration hearing and this could seriously harm your prospects of success.

Your Own Preparations for the Arbitration

Although small claims hearings are fairly informal many people find the prospect of presenting their case to the arbitrator makes them feel rather anxious. The better you prepare before the hearing the more confident you will be when you attend the arbitration.

The Plaintiff. You will have to be prepared to introduce the case to the arbitrator by telling him what it is about, what happened, why the defendant was at fault and what is at issue or in dispute. It is a good idea to write a list of important points in the order you want to mention them so that you do not forget things or repeat yourself. Look back at your particulars of claim and the defence to make sure you have not overlooked anything. If you can, find an obliging friend, practice explaining your case and ask them if what you say is clear and easy to follow.

The Defendant. You will have to respond to the plaintiff's claim however you will know in advance what this is and so will be able to predict much of what the plaintiff will say. Look at the particulars of claim and the documents you receive from the plaintiff such as expert's reports. Make a of the key allegations being made against you and then be prepared to outline your defence to the arbitrator rebutting each of these allegations. Make a list of the points you intend to make in order. You may benefit from practice in explaining your defence to a friend or relative.

Preparing to deal with witnesses. Once you have outlined your claim or defence you will have the opportunity to call witnesses to give evidence. Before the arbitration reflect on why you are calling each witness and what you hope they will say that will strengthen your case or weaken your opponents. Prepare a few questions with which you could prompt them to discuss the relevant matter without actually giving the court the evidence yourself. The arbitrator will have already heard your account of events, he now wants to hear from the witness. You may undermine the strength of his evidence if you, in effect, tell him what to say. Preparing questions in advance will help you to resist the natural temptation to try and give the witness's evidence for him.

You will also get an opportunity to question your opponent's witnesses, this is known as cross-examination.Try to think in advance of anything which weakens or discredits their evidence. For example that they could not have had a very good view of the accident, they are in business with your opponent, or their memory of events is imperfect on one point so should not be relied on in relation to another question.

In general when you are preparing for the hearing it is a good idea to try and step back from the case. This is difficult as you will naturally feel strongly about your claim or defence but if you can try and see it from an impartial viewpoint and then try and think from your opponent's perspective you may get a clearer appreciation of the strengths and weaknesses of your case and be better able to predict what will be raised at the arbitration.

It could also be worth your while trying to reach agreement with your opponent before the arbitration hearing.

CHAPTER EIGHT
SETTLING DISPUTES

It may be worth your while to try to settle the case without an arbitration hearing. This is because all litigation contains some element of risk. However much you believe in your own case there is almost always a chance that the arbitrator's decision could go against you. By reaching a settlement you save yourself the risk of losing completely in return for conceding something to your opponent.

How to Negotiate a Settlement

If you want to reach a settlement you can write to your opponent and make them an offer. Letters concerning settlements are usually headed "without prejudice". The practical effect heading your letter "without prejudice" is that if your opponent refuses your offer or ignores it then the letter and its contents cannot be used as evidence. If the offer is accepted by your opponent it becomes a binding agreement to settle the action and it can be revealed to the arbitrator. The words "without prejudice" should only be used on letters intended to assist in settling the dispute and cannot be used to make other documents inadmissible as evidence.

You could also write to your opponent and ask if they would be prepared to discuss the case on the telephone or arrange a meeting in the hope that you can negotiate a settlement. If you do not know your opponent well exercise caution and common sense and only meet them somewhere you will be safe.

When entering into negotiations it is important to be prepared. It is a good idea to write down three figures in advance. Firstly, an opening offer or request which might be slightly more than you expect to receive or less than you expect to pay, secondly the figure you would be happy to accept or to pay and thirdly your bottom line which is the minimum you would accept or the maximum you would pay your opponent.

You are free to negotiate at any time, from before the start of legal proceedings until the arbitrator makes his judgment. In small claims the disclosure of evidence normally takes place only one or two weeks before the date set for arbitration. If you feel that seeing your opponent's documents and expert's reports is likely to effect your view of the strength or weakness of their case it may be worth waiting until you have received copies before reaching any agreement.

If your opponent makes you an offer of settlement consider what his motives may be. If it is very low it could be that he has misjudged the strength of his own case but alternatively he may have spotted a genuine weakness in your case which you have not noticed. You are free to ask him why he thinks that amount is reasonable. If the offer is high you will naturally want to come to a decision quickly in case it is withdrawn but you should not necessarily accept it immediately. There may be a weakness in his case you do not yet know about or yours might be stronger than you think. If a relatively large sum is involved it might be worth taking advice on whether or not to accept it.

Consent Orders

The Court will normally approve a settlement which both sides accept. This is achieved by a Consent Order. A formal form of consent may be signed and filed with the Court any time before the hearing. In a small claim arbitration, it would be sufficient for both sides to write to the court outlining their agreement or for one party to set out the agreed compromise and the other to sign at the foot of the letter. A consent order must be approved by the judge.

At the hearing, if a compromise is agreed, the judge would record the agreement so that a consent order or judgment is drawn up by the court.

Withdrawing the Summons

If a settlement has been agreed, the plaintiff may file a Notice of Discontinuance (Form N297) and a certificate saying that the defendant has been informed of withdrawal of the Summons. The case would be ended without a court order. This option may be suitable if the Plaintiff simply abandons the case altogether, or if the defendant pays an agreed sum in one payment. If instalments are agreed, the Plaintiff is better off with a court order which is capable of enforcement. A consent order would be preferable to a discontinuance.

CHAPTER NINE
REPRESENTATION

The small claims procedure is designed with the intention that people will be able to conduct their own case and legal representation should not usually be necessary. Consequently you are allowed to have a lay representative to state your case for you, perhaps a friend or relative who feels more confident about speaking to the judge. A lay representative cannot be heard if the person he represents does not attend the hearing and the arbitrator has the right to exclude him for misconduct. If the party to the case is a company it will need the arbitrator's permission for it to be represented by anyone other than a lawyer, for example a director. Acting as a lay representative does not prevent someone from also giving evidence as a witness.

Parties to a small claim are also entitled to employ a solicitor if they wish. However they will be unable to recover the cost of legal representation from their opponent if they are successful and so they will have to pay the costs themselves. Legal aid is not normally available for representation in small claims. If a party is unable to properly represent themselves in a small claim, for example as a result of a physical disability, poor sight, pronounced stammer or inability to read, these circumstances can be taken into account by the district judge when deciding whether or not the case should be automatically referred to arbitration or whether it should go to a county court trial for which legal aid may be available. If you feel you are unable to represent yourself inform the court well before the arbitration date and ask for a preliminary appointment for directions. You could also apply for legal aid on the grounds that your circumstances are exceptional.

It is not possible to have the case sent to the county court on the grounds that one party is represented and the other is not. Inequality of representation can be worrying and intimidating for people bringing their own small claim, however it is unlikely to make a great deal of difference as the arbitrator will take a fairly active role to ensure that you are not unfairly disadvantaged by a lack of legal expertise.

CHAPTER TEN
THE ARBITRATION AND JUDGMENT PROCESS

You will receive notification of the date, time and place set for the arbitration hearing from the court when the defence has been filed. If you have not been there before allow plenty of time to find the court. What you think of as your local court may well be a magistrates court or a Crown court.

Your arbitration will be heard in the county court. You may wear what you wish but it is a good idea to dress smartly to make a favourable impression on the arbitrator. Bring the originals and spare copies of all the documents and the evidence you want to use at the hearing even though you have already sent copies to the court and your opponent.

When you arrive at court you will find a list of the days cases on a notice board. Check that your case is listed and inform the usher that you have arrived. The usher will know if your opponent has arrived and if he or she is represented by a solicitor.

Unless you have a relatively long time estimate such as a full day, cases are usually listed in blocks or groups. For example, a number of cases will be listed for 10.00 a.m. and 2.00 p.m. and will be heard in order. This means you are likely to have to spend some time waiting around before the hearing.

When it is your turn to be heard the usher will show you into the judge's room. The judge will usually be sitting at the end of a long table. You and your opponent will sit on either side. The judge will not be wearing a wig or gown and should be addressed as "Sir or Madam". Ask the judge if he would prefer the witnesses to wait outside and be called in when required, or if they may sit in on the full hearing. Only the people involved in the case will be present. Evidence is not given on oath unless the district judge directs that it should be.

Because it is the plaintiff who has brought the case to the small claims arbitration and it is the plaintiff who has made allegations or claims against the defendant it is usual for the plaintiff to begin by presenting his case at the hearing. The defendant will then have an opportunity to respond.

The plaintiff

Ask the judge if he or she has all the documents in the case such as the summons, defence, expert's reports and witness statements.

Take the judge through the list of points you have prepared or the particulars of claim to explain your case. Identify what is admitted by the defendant in the defence. This should give the judge a clear idea of what is at issue and thus what he is being asked to decide.

Having given an outline of your case introduce the evidence you have to support it. This may include your own oral evidence, documents and possibly witnesses, although this is not essential.

54

You, the judge and your opponent will all have an opportunity to question your witnesses. You will also be able to question your opponent and his witnesses.

Except when you are questioning witnesses you should address your remarks to the judge. Avoid getting involved in any direct argument with your opponent.

The Defendant

You will probably have to wait while the plaintiff presents his claims against you to the judge. You will have an opportunity to put your side later on.

When the plaintiff is speaking make a note of any important points he makes. For example if there is something you would like to question him about later or a fact that has not emerged previously.

After the plaintiff has spoken you will have the opportunity to present your defence. Use the notes you have prepared or your defence form to help you as you tell the judge all the important points.

You will have an opportunity to call your witnesses and question them as well as an opportunity to question your opponent and his witnesses.

If you have filed a Counterclaim this must be presented as though you were a plaintiff.

Whether you are a plaintiff or a defendant it is in your own best interest to remain calm and courteous throughout the hearing.

Non attendance

If the plaintiff fails to attend, the judge could decide that there is no case to answer and dismiss the summons. In such a case, the plaintiff could apply for judgment to be set aside if grounds exist. If the defendant fails to attend, the judge could enter judgment for the plaintiff or decide that there is no case to answer and dismiss the summons.

If you find you are going to be unable to attend contact the court immediately to seek an adjournment.

Making judgment

If a compromise is not possible, the judge will decide on the evidence whether the plaintiff has proved the case and is entitled to the orders requested. The judge will usually make a decision on the claim and counterclaim (if any) at the hearing. Be careful to write down what the judgment is. The court will prepare the form of judgment and serve it on both sides If it is inaccurate or incorrect, contact the court immediately.

Setting aside a Judgment

It may be possible to have judgment set aside for example. There is more information on setting aside judgments in chapter 13. It is not possible to appeal.

If judgment is made against you when you are not present, an application can be made within 14 days for judgment to be set aside and the case proceed to another arbitration. Form N244 should be used and reasons must be given.

CHAPTER ELEVEN
ENFORCING A JUDGMENT

Once you have obtained judgment on the claim or counterclaim no further action is required so long as the damages are paid. However debtors do not always comply with the court's order to pay a lump sum and may fall into arrears with payments to be made by instalments, in which case you have a number of options and can ask the court for any of the following:

A Warrant of Execution (Form N323)

This gives a bailiff the authority to visit the defendant's home or business and try to collect the money you are owed or to take goods to sell at auction. You can ask the bailiff to recover the whole amount or alternatively you can ask for part of the debt for example one or more instalments, or a minimum of £50. You cannot normally ask for a part warrant if you originally asked for the judgment to be paid in one amount. A fee will be charged and this will be added to the amount you are owed by the defendant. The fee will not be refunded if the bailiff is not able to get anything from the defendant.

To request a warrant of execution fill in form N323 and send it to the court. If you would like confirmation that the warrant has been issued you must also enclose a stamped addressed envelope. The court will send the defendant a notice to let him know that a warrant has been issued and that he must pay what is owed within seven days. If he complies the court will send the moneys on to you. If he does not the bailiff will call at his address within 15 working days of the warrant being issued to collect payment or take goods. The cost of taking and selling such goods will be deducted from the amount they raise when they are sold and then you will be sent your money.

There are limits placed on the type of goods a bailiff may take. He cannot take any items which are necessary for the basic domestic needs of the defendant and his family such as clothing or bedding or any items he requires to do his job or carry on his trade such as tools and vehicles. All property seized must belong to the defendant which means the bailiff cannot take goods which the defendant has on hire purchase, lease or which are rented, or which belong to someone else, such as the defendant's spouse. The bailiff may only take goods likely to fetch money at auction.

The bailiff is not entitled to break into the defendant's house to remove property. He may only enter with permission, however he may be able to break into the defendant's business premises if no-one is living there.

The defendant is entitled to ask that the warrant be suspended, in which case you will have a number of options. You can agree to the suspension of the warrant and accept the defendant's offer of payment, or agree to the suspension and ask that he pay more than the amount he has suggested. This would mean that a court officer would decide how much the defendant can afford to pay. Finally you can say that you do not agree to the suspension of the warrant and a hearing will be arranged.

If you object to the court officers decision about how much the defendant should pay fill in form N244 saying why you object and return it within sixteen days of the date of the postmark shown on the envelope the new order came in. A hearing will be arranged where a district judge will decide what the defendant should pay.

If the warrant is suspended but the defendant still does not pay you can use form N445 to ask the court to reissue the warrant. There is no fee for doing this. If the bailiff was unable to recover any money or goods from the defendant and have further information which means you think he should be able to then you can also reissue the warrant in these circumstances. For example, if you have a new address for the defendant or you can give details of an item the defendant owns and which would be worth selling use form N445 to inform the court.

A warrant lasts for one year. If you have still not received payment near the end of that time you should apply to extend the life of the warrant before the year ends otherwise you will have to ask for another warrant and a fee will be charged.

Attachment of Earnings (Form N337)

If the defendant is in employment, he still owes you over £50 and he is behind with his payments you may be able to get an attachment of earnings order against him. This means the court will receive payments direct from the defendants employer either monthly or weekly, depending on how he is paid and then will pass the money on to you.

To request an attachment of earnings order fill in form N337 and send it to the office of the defendant's local court with the fee. If your judgment was obtained in another court you should first write to that original court, explain that you want an attachment of earnings order and ask that the case be transferred. The defendants local court will give you a new case number and you can then send in the request form and fee. Enclose a stamped addressed envelope if you would like confirmation that your request is being dealt with.

The court will tell the defendant to pay the money owed or to fill in a form giving details of his income, expenditure and employment. A court officer will then decide how much the defendant can afford to pay having made allowance for what he needs to live on. The order will then be sent to the defendant's employer telling him what and when he should pay.

If you are not happy with the court officers decision you can use form N244 to ask for a district judge to decide what the defendant can afford to pay. You must say why you object to the decision and return the form within sixteen days of the date of the postmark shown on the envelope which the attachment of earnings order came in. A hearing will then be arranged.

The defendant is entitled to ask that the order should be suspended and that he should be allowed to make payments directly to you. If the order has been suspended and the defendant still does not pay use form N446 to request reissue of the process so that the court will send the order to his employer. No fee is charged for this.

You cannot obtain an attachment of earnings order against a defendant who is in the army, navy or air force or is a merchant seaman, a firm or a limited company. Nor can you obtain one against a defendant who is self-employed or unemployed. If the defendant is on a very low wage it might not be possible for the court to make such an order.

If the defendant has found new work after a period of unemployment during which the order had lapsed you can use form N446 to ask the court to send the attachment of earnings order to the new employer.

Garnishee Order (Form 349)

If you have obtained a judgment for more than £25 the court can order a person who owes the defendant money or who holds money on their behalf to pay you as much as is needed to cover the balance on your judgment, or if there is not sufficient to pay you as much as they have or owe.

A garnishee order can apply to most debts but is normally used to obtain money from a defendant's bank or building society accounts. You should fill in form N349 giving the name and address of the person who owes the defendant money or the name and branch of the defendant's bank if you know it. The form must then be sworn on oath. This can be done before a court officer at any county court free of charge or before a solicitor who will charge you a small fee.

There will not be a hearing. Your application will be considered by a district judge in private. If he decides to grant the order the court will send a garnishee order nisi to the person who owes or holds the money for the defendant. This person is known as the garnishee. This order will freeze the account. You will be sent a copy and the defendant will also be sent one seven days later. The delay being to stop him taking money from his account to avoid the order.

Before the money is paid to the plaintiff the defendant and the garnishee will have the opportunity to tell the court if there are any good reasons why the garnishee order nisi should not be made absolute. For example the money really belongs to someone else or the account is overdrawn. If they do not have a reason the court will make a garnishee order absolute which will mean the garnishee has to pay the money to the plaintiff.

The order only freezes the money which was held on the date when the bank or person received the order. It does not cover money paid in later.

If the defendant does not have identifiable income or money for you to claim but does own property such as a house (either freehold or leasehold) or something such as bonds, stocks and shares, you can obtain a charging order over this property. The effect would be that you would have a right to part of the value of the property and when it is sold you will receive your money.

To obtain a charging order you must prove that the debtor owns the property. In the case of land this means obtaining "Office Copy Entries" from HM Land Registry for which you will need to complete a "Public Index Map" search to find out the title number of the land.

Unlike the other types of enforcement proceedings there is no application form for a charging order. You must write and swear an affidavit saying that the defendant owes you money and giving the details. You should also say that the debt is a result of a judgment and give the date, case number and details of the judgment. State what the outstanding balance of the debt is, then send the affidavit to the court with the document from the land registry and the fee.

Once you have a charging order you can ask the court to order the defendant to sell his property to pay the debt. This is a separate procedure and you will have to issue fresh proceedings (make an originating application) and pay another fee. In practice it is difficult to obtain such an order. The court is unlikely to order the sale of a valuable property or family home to pay a small debt. You are likely to find that the defendant's home is jointly owned by his or her spouse. even if they are not registered as a legal owner a husband or wife can have rights over a house known as a "beneficial interest" which could stop you obtaining an order for sale. Furthermore the property is likely to be mortgaged and the mortgagee may well oppose the sale.

You should take advice before applying for a charging order and especially before applying for an order for sale as these procedures can be complicated and costly.

Oral Examination (Form N316)

This is not a method of enforcement but is a means of finding out information about the defendant to enable you to decide if he is able to pay you and which method of enforcement would be most appropriate. You can request an oral examination by filling in form N316 and sending it to the defendant's local court with the fee. If you obtained your judgment in a different court you must first write to that original court asking for the case to be transferred, and then send your form and fee in once this has been done.

If the defendant is a company you can request an oral examination of one of the directors. You can find out who the directors are by telephoning Companies House . The case should be transferred to the court nearest the director's home or business address rather than the one nearest to the company's registered office.

The court will send the defendant a form telling him when to attend court and instructing him to bring any documents concerning his finances. The court may also send out a questionnaire for the defendant to complete prior to the hearing.

You will be notified of when the examination is to take place. Check whether you are required to attend. If you cannot but you have specific questions which you would like the defendant to be asked write to the court and ask that they be included in the examination. You will receive a copy of the defendant's answers after the examination.

If the defendant fails to attend the examination will normally be adjourned and rescheduled for a new date. If this happens you may have to pay the defendant's reasonable travelling expenses to the attend on the new date, known as "conduct money". The defendant is entitled to ask you for this at any time up to seven days before the date fixed for the adjourned examination.

An order to attend an adjourned oral examination must be served personally by a bailiff. If the defendant fails to attend the judge can issue a warrant for his arrest provided that he is satisfied the defendant knew of the examination. The bailiff will then arrest the defendant and bring him to the court to be examined. The court will send you a copy of his answers.

Appointment of a Receiver

Receivership orders are made where it is not impossible to use any of the other legal methods of enforcement. The order will authorise the receiver to receive money, rent and profits which the judgment debtor is entitled to because of his interest in specified property. When deciding whether or not to appoint a receiver the court will take into account the amount that is owed, the amount that is likely to be obtained by a receiver and the probable costs of the appointment. It is not a usual course of action for recovering debts arising out of small claims.

An application for the appointment of a receiver must be supported by two affidavits. One stating the grounds for the order and giving details of the debt and property to be administered. The second must be sworn by an independent person who has known the receiver for at least five years and can swer that he is fit to be appointed.

Bankruptcy Proceedings

Non payment of the debt could give you grounds to issue a bankruptcy petition against the defendant. The debt must exceed £750, it must be unsecured and the debtor must either be unable to pay or have no reasonable prospect of being able to pay.

If you have begun any of the enforcement proceedings and you receive full or partial payment from the defendant you must tell the court immediately.

CHAPTER TWELVE
JUDGMENT AGAINST YOU

If you were not successful and an order has been made that you should pay your opponent you should send the payments directly to him or his representative. The name and address for payment will be shown on the court forms. You should not send payments to the court. The judgment order will tell you when to pay and if it should be by instalments. It is important that you pay on time because if you are late, even by one day, the plaintiff will be able to ask the court to take the steps outlined in the previous chapter and you are likely to have to pay the costs of such action. Always allow plenty of time for the payment to arrive. The courts recommend you allow at least four clear working days before it is due. You should pay by cheque or postal order or some other method which gives you proof you have paid. Do not send cash. You should keep a record of all the payments you make and when you send them enclose your name, address, case number and plaintiff's reference with your payment.

Setting the Judgment Aside

If you did not receive the summons and a judgment in default has been entered against you you can ask for the judgment to be set aside, which means cancelled by filling in form N244. No fee is charged. You can only ask for the judgment to be set aside on those grounds if you think that you do not have the money.

The court will arrange a hearing at which the district judge will decide whether or not to cancel the judgment. If the judgment was not made in your local court you should have the case transferred there before a hearing is arranged.

Judgments can also be set aside if there has been misconduct by the arbitrator or he made an error of law. Misconduct can include misuse of information and in some circumstances rejection of evidence or the reception of evidence in the absence of the parties.

Varying the Order

If you have been ordered to pay the whole judgment debt as one lump sum or by instalments which are too large you can use form N245 to ask the court to vary the order and reduce the payments. The plaintiff will be asked if he will agree to accept what you are offering to pay. If he will not the court will decide want you should pay. If you do not accept their decision you should write within sixteen days of the date of the postmark on the varied order giving your reasons and asking that the matter should be reconsidered. A hearing with a district judge will be arranged at your local court where the matter will be decided.

Inability to Pay money owed

If you have no income and cannot pay anything towards the debt at the moment ask the court for a stay of judgment on form N244. A hearing with a district judge will be arranged.

Suspension of Warrants and Orders

When the plaintiff tries to recover money using one of the enforcement procedures outlined in the previous chapter you will have the opportunity to apply for the warrant or order to be suspended.

Register of County Court Judgments

The judgment will be entered on the County Court Judgments Register and will remain there for six years. This may make it difficult for you to obtain credit, a mortgage or goods on hire purchase. Banks, building societies and credit companies search the Register. The Office of Fair Trading produces a booklet called "No Credit" explaining what you can do if you are refused credit.

If you pay the full amount you owe within one month of the judgment date, you can ask the court to take your name off the register. You will have to pay a fee of £3 and give the court proof that you have paid, for example a letter from the plaintiff. The court will cancel your entry on the register and give you a certificate of satisfaction which proves you paid within one month.

If you do not pay within one month you can ask the court to mark the register "satisfied" when you have paid the full amount which you owe. This will mean that anyone who searches the register will know you have paid the debt and when your last payment was made. You will receive a certificate of satisfaction but the entry will remain on the register for six years. To obtain this send the fee of £3 and proof of payment.

Administration Orders

If you have at least two outstanding debts and at least one of them is a result of a judgment you can apply to the court for an administration order using form N92. To be eligible the total sum of your debts must not be more than £5,000. The effect of an administration order would be that the court would help you to administer your finances and in the meantime none of your creditors would be able to take enforcement action or to make you bankrupt without referring to the court first.

If an administration order is made instead of paying for creditors directly you would make monthly payments to the court which would then divide the money between your creditors. The court will decide how much you have to pay after considering the information you give about your income and expenditure in your application form. You can suggest a rate at which you could pay but be realistic. Make sure it is an amount you really can afford and that you have allowed yourself enough for your basic needs.

If you have a job the court might make an order that your employer should deduct money from your earnings and send it straight to them. If you do not want this to happen indicate on your application form that you do not want an attachment of earnings order.

Fill in the form but do not sign it then take it to your local county court where you will be asked to swear on oath that the information you have given in your application is true and to sign the form in front of a court officer. If you have any documents which support your statements about your income and expenditure take them with you, for example bills and receipts.

When the court has fixed a rate of payment you and your creditors will be given 16 days in which to object. If anyone does object a hearing will be arranged.

If you have trouble paying the amount ordered contact the court immediately. If you fail to pay the court has the power to issue a warrant of execution, to make an attachment of earnings order or to revoke the administration order in which case your creditors can enforce their rights themselves. If you incur more debts after the order has been made these can only be added with the agreement of the court.

The administration order will be entered on the register of county court judgments which will mean you are likely to find it difficult to obtain credit until your debts are paid.

A Composition Order

When an administration order has been made the court may, in some circumstances, make an order that you do not have to pay the full amount which you owe. It reduces proportionately the amount owed to your various creditors.

Individual Voluntary Arrangements

You can suggest a Voluntary Arrangement which is a legally binding contract between you and your unsecured creditors. You can make a proposal for payment but it only becomes binding once the creditors have accepted it. The creditors do not have to receive the full amount due but it must be more than they would receive under your bankruptcy.

You can ask for an interim order to stay all proceedings while the creditors consider the proposal but you will need an insolvency practitioner to make the application for you which will be expensive.

Bankruptcy

An person can file his own petition to make himself bankrupt on a voluntary basis. There is a fee of £275 for this and you will need to produce a statement of affairs disclosing all assets and liabilities, and fill in a form for the court. When a debtor owes under £20,000 and is made bankrupt voluntarily rather than at the request of his creditors he may be an undischarged bankrupt for only two years rather than three.

APPENDIX 1

FORMS USED IN THE COUNTY COURT

1. DEFAULT SUMMONS-FIXED AMOUNT N1

2. DEFAULT SUMMONS-UNSPECIFIED AMOUNT N2

3. NOTICE OF ISSUE OF A DEFAULT SUMMONS AND REQUEST FOR JUDGEMENT N205A

4. FORM OF ADMISSION AND COUNTERCLAIM N9A

5. FORM OF DEFENCE AND COUNTERCLAIM N9B

6. REQUEST FOR ORAL EXAMINATION N316

7. REQUEST FOR ATTACHMENT OF EARNINGS ORDER N337

Form N1

 County Court Summons

Case Number

In the

(1)

Plaintiff's full name address

County Court

The court office is open from 10am to 4pm Monday to Friday

(2)

Address for service (and) payment
(if not as above)
Ref/Tel no.

Telephone:

Seal

(3)

Defendant's name address

This summons is only valid if sealed by the court
If it is not sealed it should be sent to the court.

What the plaintiff claims from you

Brief description of type of claim

Particulars of the plaintiff's claim against you

Amount claimed

Court fee

Solicitor's costs

Total amount

Summons issued on

What to do about this summons

You can

- dispute the claim
- make a claim against the plaintiff
- admit the claim in full and offer to pay
- pay the total amount shown above
- admit only part of the claim

For information on what to do or if you need further advice, please turn over.

Signed
Plaintiff('s solicitor)
(or see enclosed particulars of claim)

N1 Default summons (fixed amount) (Order 3, rule 3(2)(b))

Keep this summons, you may need to refer to it

76

You have 21 days from the date of the postmark to reply to this summons

(A limited company served at its registered office has 16 days to reply.)

If you do nothing	Judgment may be entered against you without further notice.
If you dispute the claim	Complete the white defence form (N9B) and return it to the court office. The notes on the form explain what you should do.
If you want to make a claim against the plaintiff (counterclaim)	Complete boxes 5 and 6 on the white defence form (N9B) and return the form to the court office. The notes at box 5 explain what you should do.
If you admit all of the claim and you are asking for time to pay	Fill in the blue admission form (N9A). The notes on the form explain what you should do and where you should send the completed form.
If you admit all of the claim and you wish to pay now	Take or send the money to the person named at box (2) on the front of the summons. If there is no address in box (2), send the money to the address in box (1). Read How to Pay below.
If you admit only part of the claim	Fill in the white defence form (N9B) saying how much you admit, then either: Pay the amount admitted as explained in the box above; or Fill in the blue admission form (N9A) if you need time to pay

Interest on Judgments

If judgment is entered against you and is for more than £5000, the plaintiff may be entitled to interest on the total amount.

Registration of Judgments

If the summons results in a judgment against you, your name and address may be entered in the Register of County Court Judgments. This may make it difficult for you to get credit. A leaflet giving further information can be obtained from the court.

Further Advice

You can get help to complete the reply forms and information about court procedures at any county court office or citizens' advice bureau. The address and telephone number of your local court is listed under "Courts" in the phone book. When corresponding with the court, please address forms or letters to the Chief Clerk. Always quote the whole of the case number which appears at the top right corner on the front of this form; the court is unable to trace your case without it.

How to pay	To be completed on the court copy only
• PAYMENT(S) MUST BE MADE to the person named at the address for payment quoting their reference and the court case number.	Served on
• DO NOT bring or send payments to the court. THEY WILL NOT BE ACCEPTED.	
• You should allow at least 4 days for your payments to reach the plaintiff or his representative.	By posting on
• Make sure that you keep records and can account for all payments made. Proof may be required if there is any disagreement. It is not safe to send cash unless you use registered post.	Officer
• A leaflet giving further advice about payment can be obtained from the court.	Marked "gone away" on
• If you need more information you should contact the plaintiff or his representative.	

Form N2

County Court Summons

	Case Number	

In the

County Court

The court office is open from 10am to 4pm Monday to Friday

Telephone

seal

This summons is only valid if sealed by the court.
If it is not sealed it should be sent to the court.

Keep this summons, you may need to refer to it.

Plaintiff's full name address

Plaintiff's Solicitor's address

Ref/Tel No.

Defendant's full name (including title e.g. Mr, Mrs or Miss) **and address**

What the plaintiff claims from you

Give brief description of type of claim

Particulars of the plaintiff's claim against you

Amount claimed	see particulars
Court fee	
Solicitor's costs	
Total Amount	

Summons issued on

What you should do

You have 21 days (16 days if you are a limited company served at your registered office) from the date of the postmark to either

- **defend the claim** by filling in the back of the enclosed form and sending it to the court;

  OR

- **admit the claim** and make an offer of payment, by filling in the front of the enclosed reply form and sending it to the court.

If you do nothing judgment may be entered against you.

My claim is worth   £5000 or less ☐   over £5000 ☐

All cases over £1000

I would like my case decided by   trial ☐   arbitration ☐

Signed
Plaintiff or plaintiff's solicitor
(or see enclosed "Particulars of claim")

N2 Default summons (amount not fixed) (Order 3, rule 3(2)(a)

Please read this page : it will help you deal with the summons

If you dispute all or part of the claim

You may be entitled to help with your legal costs. Ask about the legal aid scheme at any county court office, citizens' advice bureau, legal advice centre or firm of solicitors displaying the legal aid sign.

• Say how much you dispute in the part of the enclosed form for defending the claim and return it to the court. The court will tell you what to do next.

• If you dispute only part of the claim, you should also fill in the part of the form for admitting the claim and pay the amount admitted into court.

• If the court named on the summons is not your local county court, and/or the court for the area where the reason for the claim arose, you may write to the court named asking for the case to be transferred to the county court of your choice. You must explain your reasons for wanting the transfer. However, if the case is transferred and you later lose the case, you may have to pay more in costs.

How the claim will be dealt with if defended

If the claim is worth £1,000 or less it will be dealt with by arbitration (small claims procedure) unless the court decides the case is too difficult to be dealt with in this informal way. Costs and the grounds for setting aside an arbitration award are strictly limited. If the claim is for £1,000 or less and is not dealt with by arbitration, costs, including the costs of help from a legal representative, may be allowed.

If the claim is worth over £1000 it can still be dealt with by arbitration if either you or the plaintiff asks for it and the court approves. If your claim is dealt with by arbitration in these circumstances, costs may be allowed.

If you want to make a claim against the plaintiff

This is known as a counterclaim

Fill in the part of the enclosed form headed 'Counterclaim'. If your claim is for more than the plaintiff's claim you may have to pay a fee - the court will let you know. Unless the plaintiff admits your counterclaim there will be a hearing. The court will tell you what to do next.

If you admit the claim or any part of it

• You may pay an appropriate amount into court to compensate the plaintiff (see Payments into Court box on this page), accompanied by a notice (or letter) that the payment is in satisfaction of the claim. If the plaintiff accepts the amount paid he is also entitled to apply for his costs.

• If you need time to pay, complete the enclosed form of admission and give details of how you propose to pay the plaintiff. If your offer is accepted, the court will send an order telling you how to pay. If it is not accepted, the court will fix a rate of payment based on the details given in your form of admission and the plaintiff's comments. Judgment will be entered and you will be sent an order telling you how and when to pay.

• If the plaintiff does not accept the amount paid or offered, the court will fix a hearing to decide how much you must pay to compensate the plaintiff. The court will tell you when the hearing, which you should attend, will take place.

General information

• If you received this summons through the post the date of service will be 7 days (for a limited company at its registered office, the second working day) after the date of posting as shown by the postmark.

• You can get help to complete the enclosed form and information about court procedures at any county court office or citizens' advice bureau. The address and telephone number of your local court is listed under 'Courts' in the phone book.

• Please address forms or letters to the Chief Clerk.

• Always quote the whole of the case number which appears at the top right corner of the front of this form; the court is unable to trace your case without it.

Registration of judgments

If the summons results in a judgment against you, your name and address may be entered in the Register of County Court Judgments. This may make it difficult for you to get credit. A leaflet giving further information can be obtained from the court.

Interest on judgments

If judgment is entered against you and is for more than £5000, the plaintiff may be entitled to interest on the total amount.

Payments into Court

You can pay the court by calling at the court office which is open 10 am to 4 pm Monday to Friday

You may only pay by:
• cash
• banker's or giro draft
• cheque supported by a cheque card
• cheque (unsupported cheques may be accepted, subject to clearance, if the Chief Clerk agrees)

Cheques and drafts must be made payable to HM Paymaster General and crossed.

Please bring this form with you.

By post

You may only pay by:
• postal order
• banker's or giro draft
• cheque (cheques may be accepted, subject to clearance, if the Chief Clerk agrees).

The payment must be made out to HM Paymaster General and crossed.

This method of payment is at your own risk.

And you must:
• pay the postage
• enclose this form
• enclose a self addressed envelope so that the court can return this form with a receipt

The court cannot accept stamps or payments by bank and giro credit transfers.

Note: You should carefully check any future forms from the court to see if payments should be made directly to the plaintiff

---

To be completed on the court copy only

Served on:

By posting on:

Officer:

This summons was returned by the Post Office marked 'Gone Away' on:

N2 Default summons (amount not fixed)

N205A

Notice of Issue of Default Summons - fixed amount

To the plaintiff ('s solicitor)

Your summons was issued today. The defendant has 14 days from the date of service to reply to the summons. If the date of postal service is not shown on this form you will be sent a separate notice of service (Form N222).
The defendant may either

- Pay you your total claim.
- Dispute the whole claim. The court will send you a copy of the defence and tell you what to do next.
- Admit that all the money is owed. The defendant will send you form of admission N9A. You may then ask the court to send the defendant an order to pay you the money owed by completing the request for judgment below and returning it to the court.
- Admit that only part of your claim is owed. The court will send you a copy of the reply and tell you what to do next.
- Not reply at all. You should wait 14 days from the date of service. You may then ask the court to send the defendant an order to pay you the money owed by completing the request for judgment below and returning it to the court.

In the		
		County Court

The court office at
THE COURT HOUSE, POWIS STREET, LONDON SE18 6JW.
is open between 10 am & 4 pm Monday to Friday
Tel: 081-854 2127

Case Number	*Always quote this*	
Plaintiff *(including ref.)*		
Defendants		
Issue date		
Date of postal service		
Issue fee	£	

For further information please turn over

- -

Request for Judgment

- Tick and complete either A or B. Make sure that all the case details are given and that the judgment details at C are completed. Remember to sign and date the form. Your signature certifies that the information you have given is correct.
- If the defendant has given an address on the form of admission to which correspondence should be sent, which is different from the address shown on the summons, you will need to tell the court.

A ☐ **The defendant has not replied to my summons**
Complete all the judgment details at C. Decide how and when you want the defendant to pay. You can ask for the judgment to be paid by instalments or in one payment.

B ☐ **The defendant admits that all the money is owed**
Tick only one box below and return the completed slip to the court.

☐ I accept the defendant's proposal for payment
Complete all the judgment details at C. Say how the defendant intends to pay. The court will send the defendant an order to pay. You will also be sent a copy.

☐ The defendant has not made any proposal for payment
Complete all the judgment details at C. Say how you want the defendant to pay. You can ask for the judgment to be paid by instalments or in one payment. The court will send the defendant an order to pay. You will also be sent a copy.

☐ I do NOT accept the defendant's proposal for payment
Complete all the judgment details at C and say how you want the defendant to pay. Give your reasons for objecting to the defendant's offer of payment in the section overleaf. Return this slip to the court together with the defendant's admission N9A (or a copy). The court will fix a rate of payment and send the defendant an order to pay. You will also be sent a copy.

I certify that the information given is correct

Signed _____ Dated _____

In the	**WOOLWICH**	
		County Court
Case Number	*Always quote this*	
Plaintiff		
Defendant		
Plaintiff's Ref.		

C Judgment details
I would like the judgment to be paid

☐ (forthwith) only tick this box if you intend to enforce the order right away
☐ (by instalments of £ _____ per month)
☐ (in full by _____)

Amount of claim as stated in summons (including interest as date of issue) _____	
Interest since date of summons (if any) _____ Period _____ Rate ____ %	
Court fee as shown on summons _____	
Solicitor's costs (if any) on issuing summons ____	
Sub Total	
Solicitor's costs (if any) on entering judgment	
Sub Total	
Deduct amount (if any) paid since issue _____	
Amount payable by defendant	

N205A Notice of Issue (default summons) and request for judgment (Order 3, rule 3(2)(1), Order 9 rules 3 and 6)

80

--------------------------------- **Further Information** ---------------------------------

- The summons must be served within 4 months of the date of issue (or 6 months if leave to serve out of the jurisdiction is granted under Order 8, rule 2). In exceptional circumstances you may apply for this time to be extended provided that you do so before the summons expires.

- If the defendant does not reply to the summons or if he delivers an admission without an offer of payment you may ask for judgment. If you do not ask for judgment within 12 months of the date of service the action will be struck out. It cannot be reinstated.

- You may be entitled to interest if judgment is entered against the defendant and your claim is for more than £5000.

- You should keep a record of any payments you receive from the defendant. If there is a hearing or you wish to take steps to enforce the judgment, you will need to satisfy the court about the balance outstanding. You should give the defendant a receipt and payment in cash should always be acknowledged. You should tell the defendant how much he owes if he asks.

- You must inform the court IMMEDIATELY if you receive any payment before a hearing date or after you have sent a request for enforcement to the court.

Objections to the defendant's proposal for payment

Case Number

81

Form N9A

Admission

In the **BROMLEY** County Court

Case Number *always quote this*

Plaintiff *(including ref.)*

Defendant

When to fill in this form
- Only fill in this form if you are admitting all or some of the claim and you are asking for time to pay
- If you are disputing the claim or you wish to pay the amount claimed, read the back of the summons

How to fill in this form
- Tick the correct boxes and give as much information as you can. Then sign and date the form.
- Make your offer of payment in box 11 on the back of this form. If you make no offer the plaintiff will decide how you should pay.
- You can get help to complete this form at any county court office or citizens' advice bureau.

Where to send this form
- If you admit the claim in full
  Send the completed form to the address shown at box (2) on the front of the summons. If there is no address in box (2) send the form to the address in box (1).
- If you admit only part of the claim
  Send the form to the court at the address given on the summons, together with the white defence form (N9B).

What happens next
- If you admit the claim in full and offer to pay
  If the plaintiff accepts your offer, judgment will be entered and you will be sent an order telling you how and when to pay. If the plaintiff does not accept your offer, the court will fix a rate of payment based on the details you have given in this form and the plaintiff's comments. Judgment will be entered and you will be sent an order telling you how and when to pay.
- If you admit only part of the claim
  The court will tell you what to do next.

How much of the claim do you admit?
- ☐ I admit the full amount claimed as shown on the summons **or**
- ☐ I admit the amount of £ ___

1 Personal details

Surname ___

Forename ___

☐ Mr ☐ Mrs ☐ Miss ☐ Ms
☐ Married ☐ Single ☐ Other *(specify)*

Age ___

Address ___

Postcode ___

2 Dependants *(people you look after financially)*

Number of children in each age group

under 11 ___ 11-15 ___ 16-17 ___ 18 & over ___

Other dependants *(give details)* ___

3 Employment

☐ I am employed as a ___

My employer is ___

Jobs other than main job *(give details)* ___

☐ I am self employed as a ___

Annual turnover is.................. £ ___

☐ I am not in arrears with my national insurance contributions, income tax and VAT

☐ I am in arrears and I owe.......... £ ___

Give details of:
(a) contracts and other work in hand ___
(b) any sums due for work done ___

☐ I have been unemployed for ___ years ___ months

☐ I am a pensioner

4 Bank account and savings

☐ I have a bank account
  ☐ The account is in credit by .... £ ___
  ☐ The account is overdrawn by.... £ ___

☐ I have a savings or building society account
  The amount in the account is .... £ ___

5 Property

I live in
☐ my own property
☐ jointly owned property
☐ rented property
☐ lodgings
☐ council property

N9A Form of admission and statement of means to accompany Form N1 (order 9, rule2) (1.95)   N9A 152   Printed by Satellite Press Limited

Form N9A Continued

6 Income

My usual take home pay *(including overtime, commission, bonuses etc)*	£	per
Income support	£	per
Child benefit(s)	£	per
Other state benefit(s)	£	per
My pension(s)	£	per
Others living in my home give me	£	per
Other income *(give details below)*		
	£	per
	£	per
	£	per
Total income	£	per

7 Expenses

(Do not include any payments made by other members of the household out of their own income)

I have regular expenses as follows:

Mortgage *(including second mortgage)*	£	per
Rent	£	per
Council Tax	£	per
Gas	£	per
Electricity	£	per
Water charges	£	per
TV rental and licence	£	per
HP repayments	£	per
Mail order	£	per
Housekeeping, food, school meals	£	per
Travelling expenses	£	per
Children's clothing	£	per
Maintenance payments	£	per
Others *(not court orders or credit debts listed in boxes 9 and 10)*		
	£	per
	£	per
	£	per
Total expenses	£	per

8 Priority debts *(This section is for arrears only. Do not include regular expenses listed in box 7.)*

Rent arrears	£	per
Mortgage arrears	£	per
Council Tax/Community Charge arrears	£	per
Water charges arrears	£	per
Fuel debts: Gas	£	per
Electricity	£	per
Other	£	per
Maintenance arrears	£	per
Others *(give details below)*		
	£	per
	£	per
Total priority debts	£	per

9 Court orders

Court Case No.	£	per
Total court order instalments	£	per

Of the payments above, I am behind with payments to *(please list)*

10 Credit debts

Loans and credit card debts *(please list)*

	£	per
	£	per
	£	per

Of the payments above, I am behind with payments to *(please list)*

11 Do you wish to make an offer of payment?

- *If you take away the totals of boxes 7, 8 and 9 and the payments you are making in box 10 from the total in box 6 you will get some idea of the sort of sum you should offer. The offer you make should be one you can afford.*

☐ I can pay the amount admitted on

or

☐ I can pay by monthly instalments of £

12 Declaration   I declare that the details I have given above are true to the best of my knowledge

Signed _____   Dated _____

Position *(firm or company)* _____

Form N9B

Defence and Counterclaim

When to fill in this form
- Only fill in this form if you wish to dispute all or part of the claim and/or make a claim against the plaintiff (counterclaim).

How to fill in this form
- Please check that the correct case details are shown on this form. You must ensure that all the boxes at the top right of this form are completed. You can obtain the correct names and numbers from the summons. The court cannot trace your case without this information.
- Follow the instructions given in each section. Tick the correct boxes and give the other details asked for.
- If you wish only to make a claim against the plaintiff (counterclaim) go to section 5.
- Complete and sign section 6 before returning this form.

Where to send this form
- Send or take this form immediately to the court office at the address shown above.
- If you admit part of the claim and you are asking for time to pay, you will also need to fill in the blue admission form (N9A) and send both reply forms to the court.
- Keep the summons and a copy of this defence; you may need them.

Legal Aid
- You may be entitled to legal aid. Ask about the legal aid scheme at any county court office, Citizens Advice Bureau, legal advice centre or firm of solicitors displaying the legal aid sign.

What happens next
- If you complete box 3 on this form, the court will ask the plaintiff to confirm that he has received payment. If he tells the court that you have not paid, the court will tell you what you should do.
- If you complete box 4 or 5, the court will tell you what you should do.
- If the summons is not from your local county court, it will automatically be transferred to your local court.

1 How much of the claim do you dispute?

☐ I dispute the full amount claimed (go to section 2)

or

☐ I admit the amount of £ _____

If you dispute only part of the claim you must either:

- pay the amount admitted to the person named at the address for payment in box (2) on the front of the summons or if there is no address in box (2), send the money to the address in box (1) (see How to Pay on the back of the summons). Then send this defence to the court.

or

- complete the blue admission form and this defence form and send them to the court.

Tick whichever applies

☐ I paid the amount admitted on (date) _____

or

☐ I enclose the completed form of admission

(go to section 2)

In the   **BROMLEY**   **County Court**

Case Number _Always quote this_ _____

Plaintiff (including ref.)

Defendant

The court office is open from 10am to 4pm Monday to Friday

COLLEGE ROAD,
BROMLEY, KENT, BR1 3PX
Telephone: 0181 464 9727

2 Arbitration under the small claims procedure

How the claim will be dealt with if defended

If the total the plaintiff is claiming is £3,000 or less, it will be dealt with by arbitration (small claims procedure) unless the court decides the case is too difficult to be dealt with in this informal way. Costs and the grounds for setting aside an arbitration award are strictly limited. If the claim is not dealt with by arbitration, costs, including the costs of help from a legal representative, may be allowed.

If the total the plaintiff is claiming is more than £3,000, it can still be dealt with by arbitration if you or the plaintiff ask for it and the court approves. If your claim is dealt with by arbitration in these circumstances, costs may be allowed.

Please tick this box if you would like the claim dealt with by arbitration. ☐
(go on to section 3)

3 Do you dispute this claim because you have already paid it? Tick whichever applies

☐ No (go to section 4)

☐ Yes I paid £ _____ to the plaintiff

on _____ (before the summons was issued - see summons)

Give details of where and how you paid it in the box below (then go to section 6)

Case No. [   ]

4 If you dispute the claim for reasons other than payment, what are your reasons?

Use the box below to give full details *(If you need to continue on a separate sheet, put the case number in the top right hand corner)*

[ ]

5 If you wish to make a claim against the plaintiff (counterclaim)

If your claim is for a specific sum of money, how much are you claiming? £ [   ]

* If your claim against the plaintiff is for more than the plaintiff's claim against you, you may have to pay a fee. Ask at your local court office whether a fee is payable.

* You may not be able to make a counterclaim where the plaintiff is the Crown (eg a Government Department). Ask at your local county court office for further information.

What are your reasons for making the counterclaim?

* Use the box opposite to give full details. *(If you need to continue on a separate sheet, put the case number in the top right hand corner.)*

(go on to section 6)

6 Signed
(To be signed by you or by your solicitor)

Position *(if signing on behalf of firm or company)*

Give an address to which notices about this case can be sent to you

Postcode [   ]

Dated

Form N316

Request for Oral Examination

to be completed and signed by the plaintiff or his solicitor and sent to the court with the appropriate fee

1 Plaintiff's name and address

In the

County Court

Case Number

2 Name and address for service and payment (if different from above) Ref/Tel No.

For court use only

O/E no.

Issue date:

3 Defendant's name and address

Hearing date:

on

at   o'clock

at (address)

4 Name and address of person to be orally examined if different from Box 3

(ie director of defendant company)

5 Judgment details

Court where judgment/order made if not court of issue

I apply for an order that the above defendant (the officer of the defendant company named in Box 4) attend and be orally examined as to his (the defendant company's) financial circumstances and produce at the examination any relevant books or documents

6 Outstanding debt

you may be able to claim interest if judgment entered for more than £5000 on or after 1 July 1991

Balance of debt and any interest*/damages at date of this request

Issue fee

AMOUNT NOW DUE

Unsatisfied warrant costs

I certify that the balance now due is as shown

Signed

Plaintiff (Plaintiff's solicitor)

Dated

IMPORTANT
You must inform the court immediately of any payments you receive after you have sent this request to the court

N316 Request for oral examination (Order 25, rule 3(1A)

Request for Attachment of Earnings Order

to be completed and signed by the plaintiff or his solicitor and sent to the court with the appropriate fee

1 Plaintiff's name and address	**In the**
	County Court
	Case Number
2 Name and address for service and payment (if different from above) Ref/Tel No.	*for court use only* **A/E application no.** Issue date: Hearing date:
3 Defendant's name and address	on at o'clock at (address)

4 Judgment details

Date of judgment/order

Court where judgment/order made if not court of issue

5 Outstanding debt

Balance due at date of this request

Issue fee

AMOUNT NOW DUE

Unsatisfied warrant costs

I apply for an attachment of earnings order

I certify that the whole or part of any instalments due under the judgment or order have not been paid and the balance now due is as shown

Signed

Plaintiff (Plaintiff's solicit.

Dated

Please proceed with this application in my absence (delete if for maintenance or otherwise appropriate)

6 Employment Details *(please give as much information as you can)*

Employer's name and address

Defendant's place of work (if different from employer's address)

The defendant is employed as

Works No/Pay Ref.

IMPORTANT
You must inform the court immediately of any payments you receive after you have sent this request to the court

APPENDIX 2

EXAMPLE PARTICULARS OF CLAIM

PARTICULARS OF CLAIM

1. The defendants are and were at all times in the business of building work generally.

2. On the 14th June 1997 the defendants in the course of their business contracted with the plaintiff to build an extension to their home, at a price of £9,000.

3. It was an inplied term of the contract that:

the extension would be finished within 2 months of work commencing;

that there would be a three month guarantee period;

that the price was fixed at £9,000.

4. On the 19th July 1997 the plaintiff was informed that the work would now cost £11,000 due to unforeseen difficulties and that the timescale would now be four months.

5. The defendants further said that if the plaintiff did not accept the terms offered then they would cease work immediatly and further, they would restore the building to its original state.

6. By reasons of the matters aforesaid the plaintiff has suffered loss and damage.

PARTICULARS OF LOSS

1. Deposit withheld £2,000

2. Cost of restoring back addition of house to original £2,000.

3. And the plaintiff claims

1) Damages
2) Interest
3) Costs

DEFENCE AND COUNTERCLAIM

1. It is denied that the defendants were in breach of the said implied terms as alleged in the particulars of claim. In particular it stated that the plaintiffs were in full possession of the facts in that the defendants informed them that there may be additional work to the extension which might incur further charges. Also, the defendants made clear that the monies paid at the outset of works would be witheld in the event of any problems. The monies would cover any works to date. Costs of restoring the building to the original would be extra.

Counterclaim

The defendant is claiming additional monies from the plaintiff for restoring the extension to its original state and is also claiming damages and compensation for lost work time.

Other titles in the Easyway Series:

Guide to Letting Property.
Guide to Bankruptcy and Insolvency
Guide to Buying and Selling a Home
Writing your C.V-Conducting an Effective interview
Guide to Employment Law

Forthcoming:

Guide to Family Law
Guide to Consumer Law
Guide to Effective Business planning
Bookkeeping and Accounts for Small Business
How to Start your own Business.

If You would like to comment on this book or to
contribute a title to the series please contact:

Easyway Guides
38 Cromwell Rd
Walthamstow
London E17 9JN.